The Collectivistic Premise

The Collectivistic Premise

Economics in a New Key

Eli Merchant

AuthorHouse™ LLC
1663 Liberty Drive
Bloomington, IN 47403
www.authorhouse.com
Phone: 1-800-839-8640

Published by AuthorHouse   02/20/2014

ISBN: 978-1-4817-2146-2 (sc)
ISBN: 978-1-4817-2145-5 (e)

Library of Congress Control Number: 2013903667

To Diana

CONTENTS

❧ PREFACE ❧

It may be opportune at this moment in history to begin the reassessment of our most basic assumptions and premises concerning human and economic behavior. This is not an easy task either for an individual or society at large. An individual will usually not question the premises or assumptions motivating his conduct, or even be aware of them, until experience forces him to do so when his actions produce consequences that do not match his expectations and may in fact go counter to them. Even then he may decide to experience these frustrations in adhesion to previous practice if they do not totally interfere with his modus operandi. However if they occur often enough and exact a sufficiently costly toll, he will have to rethink his course of action and modify his behavior accordingly, beginning the difficult process of self-examination involved.

Are we culturally, sociologically and above all economically at a similarly crucial point in our policies and the ways we look at the world? Are we facing obstacles and impediments particularly now that the globe has shrunk and geographic distances no longer matter, or matter as profoundly in the way they did previously, sabotaging the assumptions and premises clung to for generations in shaping our economic practices and beliefs?

Let us look at some of these assumptions and premises.

It is generally accepted by many economists that humans are actuated by self-interest at least in the economic sphere. But is it true in an absolute universal sense? Are there no exceptions to this principle? Does not experience provide us with daily examples of regressive and destructive behavior that defy all rational utilitarian calculations and belie this principle? If we look at institutions military, ecclesiastic, eleemosynary, cultural, artistic, and the people who populate them, the soldier ready to sacrifice his life for his country, the philanthropist genuinely devoted to eradicating social wrongs, the artist who will forego economic rewards to remain true to his artistic vision, the nun and monk who forsake worldly satisfactions, we realize that the paradigm of self-interest is no more acceptable than the opposite premise underlying so much of discredited Communist ideology of human perfectibility where the individual can shed his bourgeois instincts for the greater good.

Another premise is that the nation state can control economic events and phenomena within the market place, and that through the appropriate regulative action can shelter its citizenry from the economic storms that interfere with the fulfillment of its function. However, given the globalization of commerce where every part of the world is a part of a larger mosaic, it is unlikely that any nation state can perform this function in any genuine and effective sense. Hence the arguments between conservative and liberal theories concerning regulation and its role in the economy seem academic and irrelevant. Whether the state should or should not take measures to regulate the economy becomes increasingly academic, that is, if the state does not have the means to successfully implement these measures. In fact, are political entities known as "states" that emerged in post-feudal Europe where an agricultural economy gave way to an industrial one still relevant and meaningful in today's world? Or are they going the way of the dinosaur given the emergence of a new global economic environment?

The same can be said of the nation state from a military point of view. It was not that long ago when a country like Germany and Japan could entertain with some degree of plausibility and credibility, at least as far as its peoples were concerned, military ventures that would result in the domination of other parts of the world. What was the point of these military ventures? Was it defense of national interests? Was it attainment of economic advantage? Was it political and ideological domination in and for itself? It is interesting to note that even small nations like Belgium and Holland, which now seem the embodiment of democracy and neutrality, sought militaristic ventures to advance their economic agendas in former times in their conquest of the Congo and Indonesia. All of this seems so remote, implausible and unreal in the world as constituted today where war provides no advantage either for the aggressor or the victim nation that it is hard to reconstruct the motivation that led nations to these policies to begin with.

A person like a Caesar and Alexander, Genghis Kahn or Attila the Hun, Napoleon or Hitler seems as remote as a prehistoric species from a distant past.

It is interesting moreover that the most fundamental threat to global peace is a stateless creature, Al Qaeda, operating outside conventional geographical boundaries.

There have been important climacteric moments in the lives of people and nations. One occurred when man shifted from land to oceanic transportation as Columbus took his three ships from Spain to the New World and opened up a new dimension in human history.

Are we now at a new point in human evolution when galactic space opens to us and demands a new realignment of socio-political relations on earth?

The question has sometimes been raised as to what would happen if an extraterrestrial foe appeared from outer space. Would that help unite us earthlings in all our infinite divisions against a common extra terrestrial enemy? Was that what happened in the United States when the common enemy Japan and Germany united all Americans whatever their political ideologies? Is that what happened when we engaged in wars every twenty or thirty years as the collectivizing forces of war countered and neutralized the anti-collectivizing forces manifesting themselves during peacetime that threatened the harmonious existence of the Union? Are conflict and the concept of the "other" which it entails the only means of achieving social cohesion and a sense of community? The answer to the question could prove a fruitful basis of further study.

❧ INTRODUCTION ❧

In the following pages, we will attempt to formulate the basis of what Adam Smith calls a "nation's wealth."

Taking our country as an example, we cannot speak of the vast acreage of our country as the source of its wealth. If acreage were the sole determinant, Siberia, Canada, Brazil would obviously be superior to us in this regard.

Neither can we think of the wealth hidden in our soil, whether in terms of mineral ore or oil deposits, forestry, or agriculture as the source of wealth though it must be admitted that we have been incredibly blessed in this respect.

Climate and environmental factors play a role too as they may have figured in the emergence of the earliest societies in Egypt and Babylon but even these are not of ultimate importance.

Rather, we postulate that the essence of the wealth is the "collectivistic" spirit driving its people in their economic pursuits, and it is the analysis of the collectivistic spirit which will be the basis of our study.

It may be useful and interesting to compare the difference of the colonization of America by the English and the Spaniards in this respect. The objectives of the militaristic ventures of the Spanish conquistadores were essentially the accumulation of gold and precious metals. They were very successful in this regard, accumulating treasures beyond compare. But ultimately the tremendous influx of gold into Spain and its inflationary consequences had a totally negative and devastating effect on its economy as well as its political fortunes and prevented it from achieving the prominence which its overseas acquisitions would seem to have entitled it to in comparison to other European nations.

On the other hand, the English colonists came essentially to North America to seek the opportunities which a new beginning in cooperation with others would produce. As the country grew, these opportunities were then extended to other European immigrants, and in the twentieth century to immigrants from Africa and Asia as well. As a consequence, the nation achieved the greatest accumulation of wealth in human history, demonstrating the principle that the source of wealth lies not in gold or material things but in the collectivistic spirit uniting people economically in a mutual quest for expansion and growth.

In describing the collectivistic premise that creates wealth in the following pages, we must admit that it is not a static but dynamic force that can shrink and expand, and can be countered as history amply demonstrates by anti-collectivistic forces not easily recognized as such. Thus, citing again our own country as an example, we would do the facts an injustice if we neglected to mention that the enhancement of the white race from Europe was bought at the expense of the Native American Indians and through the enslavement of Black people from Africa or if we overlooked the numerous periodic wars that ritualistically characterized American history from its founding days to the present. This dark or negative side like the human sacrifices of old which were meant to bring down benedictions on the Aztec and Mayan inhabitants of the continent and appease the angry gods must be acknowledged as part of our own history as well.

In describing the emergence and flowering of the collectivistic premise, we must not forget the role and function of the artist who sometimes is seen as marginal and even inimical to the world of commerce and trade. In the story "Witch's Money" by Collier which we will cite at greater length later it is interesting to see how the arrival of the artist totally transforms a backward village from a dull semi-impoverished, reclusive community to an enterprising, prosperous and flourishing one as he indirectly and unexpectedly stimulates and awakens their collectivistic sense of unity—a role often played by imaginative individuals (whether we call them "artist" or not or by any other designation is not relevant) who could bring out the potential of people in a way they may not have been aware of. The role of imagination, metaphor and illusion should not be forgotten which is like a seed that can bear unexpectedly fruitful results, transforming barrenness and sterility to fruition and productivity.

The following pages will attempt to develop, formulate and expound the collectivistic premise in regard to the concept of commodities, work, and trade that have played such an important role in the marketplace, and determine to what degree it can be reconciled with the opposite forces of anti-collectivism at this critical juncture in human history where globalism replaces the nation state as the driver of economic phenomena and technological development seems to be improving life on the one hand and yet constitutes great threats and dangers to it on the other.

❧ CHAPTER I ❧

The Market Place

What is meant by the "marketplace"? The word
has been used in economic language regularly in today's
world, but has never been defined per se. Generally
much depends on the ideological perspective from
which it is viewed, providing a justification of whatever
conclusions one intends to derive from it in advance.
Obviously a liberal who believes that governmental
regulation and intervention is desirable and even
necessary in the operations of the market place will have
one view—a conservative who would like to see as little
intervention and regulation as possible will have another.
It is doubtful that as in other sciences—and economics
at least in modern times does make claim to a scientific

status—the concept will have a fixed meaning to which all can agree.

Perhaps the best way to begin the study of economics is as Adam Smith, the founder and father of economic thought who first approached economics from an empirical and scientific perspective, and whose ideas still have relevance to today's world, did from a psychological and motivational perspective. Why do people join the marketplace? Economic behavior is ultimately only one aspect of human behavior which like any other can benefit from a psychological perspective in its study and analysis. As Smith's parable of the brewer, baker, and butcher suggests, the people who are involved in economic negotiations in the market place pursue their economic activity not out of altruistic concern for others, but purely out of self-interest since this is the means whereby they can satisfy their individual needs and desires. Such self-interest however is not destructive. It is the most efficacious means whereby people can gratify their own needs in harmonization with those of others and maximize the output of products and services the market can deliver and achieve that genuine coherence and unity which would otherwise have been impossible to attain.

It is not from the benevolence of the butcher, the brewer, or the baker that we expect our dinner, but from their regard to their own interest. We address ourselves, not to their humanity, but to their self-love, and never talk to them of our own necessities, but of their advantages.

This is not to say that the butcher, baker and brewer cannot pursue philanthropic activities. Some of the wealthiest moguls and magnates such as the Vanderbilts and Rockefellers, or the Gates and Buffets of more recent times, have donated huge amounts of their fortunes to social and public objectives, and it is hard to think of our modern environment and the tremendous enrichments that characterize it (architecture, libraries, museums, parks, research grants, universities, hospitals, etc.) without their efforts that have brought these about. Nor is it to deny that philanthropic and charitable associations can help channel this donated wealth to its appropriate objectives. But this does not get to the root of the matter that it is in the belly of the marketplace where the forces driving economic activity operate and are driven by purely selfish considerations that we must look for the origins of economic activity and the wealth this produces.

Perhaps another way of stating this is that the term "economic man" does not describe the behavior of every human being—the ascetic who renounces worldly pleasures, the soldier who sacrifices his life for the welfare of society, the philanthropist who puts the needs of others in front of his own, the criminal who pursues his destructive aims whatever the consequences, and other individuals who seem to flout the norms of conventional behavior—but statistically given the enormous range of the market itself and its participants the concept of self-interest will lead and guide us accurately in determining the reasons for the conduct of the average market constituent, and is the ultimate factor which the scientific economist seeing things as they are not as they should be must take into account in his projections and calculations.

Let us examine this premise further. While it may seem on the surface that the baker, brewer and butcher are motivated by purely personal needs is it not possible that they are also driven by social and collectivistic needs? and by the need essentially to cooperate with others not only as a means but also as an end in and of itself? Is it not true as we shall examine more fully later that the products and services they render to society are conditioned by the very society and marketplace they inhabit and operate in and that such products and services may be unknown or even antithetical to the guiding spirit and values characterizing other marketplaces? Instead of the marketplace being understood as the sum total of the individuals in it whether in the activities of consumption, or work, or trade, it may be more appropriate to view their activities as being determined by it.

Mathematicians assure us that mathematical entities can be understood both by integral and differential calculus. One looks at the totality, the other at the parts that constitute it. The same approach should be used to understanding the market place which having been viewed as the sum total of all the living beings operating in it constitutes in turn a creature in its own right larger than and transcending these individuals.

Sociologically and politically, wherever we discover the existence of humans we see the existence of the group. There is no time when as the social contract theorists of the Age of Enlightenment predicated (the time when Adam Smith formulated his theories) men lived as individuals in a state of nature and then voluntarily banded together and formed the contractual agreements constituting the beginnings of organized society.

The same is true of the market place. There is no time in history when human beings lived alone and then banded out of utilitarian purposes in a market place to gratify their individual needs, their needs being molded by the very market place which they are thought to have originated. Every marketplace to the degree that markets can be thought of as historically and geographically distinct has its own character and personality. To some degree, and this is of course truer in the economic realm ushered in during the Modern Age as opposed to Medieval times, certain individuals can change and transform the marketplace. Hence the possibility of a Gutenberg, an Edison, a Rockefeller, a Gates or a Jobs to modify the parameters of the market place and impose their vision and individual perspectives on it. But still they come into the marketplace as something inherited from the past, and which as changed by their actions will endure into the future. The concept of a self-sufficient Robinson Crusoe as the prototype of the economic man motivated by purely utilitarian motives is interesting as fiction, nothing more.

Before proceeding with examples we may attend to questions of geographical, historical, ethical and political dimensions in the marketplace and the roles these play.

What about geographical limits? Can markets be distinguished from one another in the sense that we speak of a French or German—or more accurately of a European—economy as separate from an American economic one? From time immemorial, long before technology transformed our concept of the world, no market functioned in total isolation. In the ancient world, the Silk Road linked the Roman Empire to the economies of Asia, working to the economic benefit and advantage of both. Columbus' voyage was propelled by a quest for more expedient trade routes to the Far East and the products Medieval Europe enjoyed. In pre-Columbian American, trade occurred amongst its neighboring tribes and nations where the arts of war intermingled with those of commerce and where traders often enjoyed the immunity we grant to foreign ambassadors.

What about historical boundaries? Is the present moment in which the economist views the market the only significant criterion in evaluating it? Obviously the marketplace must extend over a period of time for many of its objectives to materialize. In assessing it, one must take into consideration the effects of present ventures and projects on the future. And one must also look retrospectively to actions and activities of previous generations that made the economical situation of the present possible. How far back and forth should such historical consciousness go? The building of the great cathedrals in Medieval Europe spanned many centuries, uniting workers not only across geographical but historical lines as they saw themselves as a smaller component of a larger economic framework stretching over large periods of time. Our educational systems, elementary schools, high school, colleges and universities ensure that the economic benefits we enjoy will be relayed to the future. Holidays, particularly Christmas that is the nub of economic activity in the United States and without which its economy could not thrive as it does, rest essentially on the basis of historical continuity.

To what extent do ethical considerations relate to the concept of economics? Is it foreign or intrinsic as was once thought? Ethics and science do not of course mix. A Darwin, Freud or Einstein does not impose an ethical frame on the phenomena he studies. It is the abandonment of an ethical perspective for one of total neutrality and objectivity that gives legitimacy to their findings. It is not what they personally think of the facts that matters—but the facts themselves that can be chronicled, documented and eventually shared with others. Yet if the collectivist premise implies that the agora or the market place is intrinsically an interactive place where individual destinies are bound up with one another in a larger communal context it is possible that the ethical intervention may not be a totally foreign one but that it may prove an indispensible means of understanding it.

Finally, it behooves us to add that the marketplace or the agora cannot be distinguished from the political marketplace where discussion about its nature must be discussed and evaluated. It is interesting that in ancient Greece the word "agora" suggested both these meanings. Decisions concerning the market place cannot be made from above by those who hold the political strings—whether as in Communist countries now in decline throughout the world where these were formulated by commissars and Communist higher-ups—or by theologians in the Middle Ages who decided which economic activities were legitimate as opposed to which were not—or in Capitalist countries that seem ostensibly democratic but where those with enormous power and wealth can exert unparalleled advantage in determining the character and direction of the market place. Rather as many people as possible must join the political conversation shaping the marketplace if it is to fulfill its integrative role and function in an authentic and, above all, collectivistic manner.

❧ CHAPTER II ❧

Consumption: The Concept of Commodity

The concept of a commodity, the starting point for many economists in formulating their theories, can be defined in two ways. One focuses on the work put into it, it being understood that in its finalized form it may represent all kinds of accretions of labor that have gathered on top of one another in the process of its production. From another point of view, value or utility is its defining feature. Obviously both factors are of ultimate significance. A dug ditch that may represent hours, days, and months of work is from an economic point of view worthless since it does not reflect value or use to customers in the market place. On the other hand, air is one of the most important elements on which human survival depends, having inimitable value, yet since it does not involve work at least not in our present environment it cannot be said to achieve a commodity status.

Yet there is another way of looking at the commodity in terms of promoting social and communal cohesiveness. Let us take a look at the dining experience in a restaurant, which has become such a favorite pastime of Americans today, without distinguishing between a commodity that has a physical body and form and a service that cannot be quantified in terms of weight, height, length and width and perishes according to Adam Smith in the instant of its performance. Now obviously the dining experience is driven by the imperatives of physical hunger which an individual diner shares with all human beings and even animal creatures. However, the pangs of hunger cannot be that intense to where one wolfs the food down as quickly as possible when the dining experience is meant to be savored in a slow methodic manner where every morsel can have a relished impact. Nor can one of course approach the meal in a state of satiety. Hunger in the right degree is an essential pre-condition for a meal's enjoyment as indulgence must be mixed with renunciation in the right proportions.

There are obviously many elements in the dining experience that motivate a person to eating out. There are esthetic considerations like the restaurant's ambience and decor, the friendliness of the waiters, the culinary creativity and artfulness of the chef. But what cannot be stressed enough is the presence of other people—whether the group one sits down with and engages in a conversation—or the strangers at other tables whom one does not know, yet forming a transient but genuine sense of community. Without the social environment to which the food connects us, the meal would not prove a source of positive gratification, suggesting human isolation, a state of "hunger" understood in a communal rather than biological sense. Witness the effect of a Hopper painting in this respect showing the desolation involved in a lonely dining setting, as the viewer fills in the sense of community that should have been there but is starkly lacking.

Such a sense of community is enhanced say at times like Thanksgiving when one shares the meal centering around a turkey not only with one's family and the restaurant's clientele but in fact with people far outside the geographical confines of the restaurant involving Americans spread out all over the continent. In other words, the eating of the turkey however well prepared, gratifying, and nutritious would not be indulged in were it not for the fact that millions are eating it on the same day as it forms a symbolic link connecting them in a gratifying and meaningful manner.

Beyond that, the collectivist premise expresses itself not only geographically but historically as we connect with past as well as future generations when we both look wistfully back at the experiences of our childhood and eagerly anticipate those of the generations to come, linking us into a larger historical whole, and without which the meal would not have the richly gratifying symbolic value it possesses.

A similar example can be drawn from the Seder meal that observant Jews engage in over the entire world wherever they are situated, and also share in common with the generations before them as well as those succeeding them, rooted in the mythological moment when they had succeeded in escaping bondage in Egypt in their flight to the Promised Land.

Further examples can be found in other national, religious and ethnic groups where food plays a ritualistic and symbolic rather than purely biological function.

This may be the reason the wells of compassion are opened at such holidays—not only because we feel the physical pain and duress of the hungry, which is just as intense as at any other moment of the year—but essentially because the principle of collectivity which is asserted at this time of the year is violated and rent asunder by those who cannot participate in it, whose "hunger" is not of a biological but sociological nature. As the Hagaddah, the narratological counterpart of the Seder ritual exclaims: "Let all who are hungry come and eat; let all who are needy come and celebrate the Passover with us," enunciating a precept embraced by most modern religions, the "hunger" in the context arising from an essentially spiritual origin.

Let us analyze the dining experience further in terms of our collectivistic needs by pointing out that if a society is united by the foods it prefers it is also united by those it rejects and considers taboo. If much of the world does not adhere to the rigid strictures enumerated in the Old Testament concerning what is and is not edible, there are still foods many find abhorrent or objectionable from a modern perspective because of socio-psychological tastes and attitudes, environmental concerns or other considerations. It is doubtful that many people in Western societies would find insects or endangered species a palatable source of nutrition, or ever look at the eating of horses, dogs and cats for whom we have developed a special affection as anything but repellent. Similarly the prohibition of drugs, marijuana, opium, cocaine, etc., whose use has reached such critical proportions in modern times while anchored in medical reasons may reflect the perpetual conflict between suppression and hedonism recast in a contemporary form.

Furthermore, to return to our model of dining out the collectivist principle involving the consumption of food is demonstrated by the following:

* The traditional order in which food is eaten as subsumed under the categories of appetizers, main course, desert giving the meal a structural and almost dramatic form and organization characteristic of a specific culture but not necessarily of any another

* The time of day when the meal is partaken, breakfast, lunch, dinner, and the foods in turn appropriate for these

* The dishes as well as the utensils, silverware, tablecloth, napkins, etc., with which food and drink are properly eaten and drunk and the formalities of etiquette prescribed in their consumption

It is interesting in this regard that the principle of renunciation which is part and parcel of the dining experience can result in the seemingly enigmatic result that a fast day like Yom Kippur for Jews or Ramadan for Muslims gratifies the collectivistic "hunger' at the expense of the biological one.

There are many other areas in which the collectivist premise asserts itself. While it is impossible in the confines of these pages to study each one exhaustively, let us look at some of them from this perspective.

CLOTHING. As the story of the Garden of Eden suggests, clothing is not always associated with a protection against the elements—that is one of its purposes but not the only one. During the centuries, it has undergone numerous modifications some of which from the perspective of the present seem weird and absurd: Witness the corset that suffocated the life out of women to achieve a superhuman slenderness or the peruke that weighed a ton upon the aristocratic head and necessitated help to carry it. No doubt future generations may view our clothing with similar surprise, like the tie, say, the little piece of cloth dangling from a man's neck in accompaniment to the business suit, which does nothing to defend him against the exigencies of the weather, yet is indispensible in projecting a sense of responsibility appropriate for office work or gaining social acceptance—or the wedding gown that climaxes every woman's dreams and aspirations and consumes enormous amount of money and time, but is designed to last only one night.

It is interesting that even in a particular geographical area or historical period clothing may differ from context to context—and what is appropriate in one may not be so in another. A person would be out of place in his working clothes at a wedding or formal situation—and on the other hand, a man in formal attire may feel totally out of place in a relaxed informal situation. To take an extreme example, similar to the one of fasting mentioned before, the fully dressed man and woman may feel "naked" in a nudist colony.

Ethnic and religious clothing may often acquire a symbolic meaning and significance that may not always be fully comprehended and appreciated by outside groups and often can cause irrational fear and anxiety and even lead to persecution and attack: The Amish in their simple almost austere attire; the Chasidic Jew in apparel that harks back to previous centuries; the priest, monk or nun in their ecclesiastical garb, etc.

HOUSING. Like clothing, housing protects us from external dangers, yet also serves collectivistic needs. In contrast to the theory of the State of Nature current in the eighteenth century that individuals at first lived alone and subsequently united to form society, it is far more probable that from the earliest time homes providing shelter were in close proximity to one another, constituting a collective space, whether in the village, town, or city, enabling commerce and social intercourse. As technology developed it was possible for homes to spread across ever wider geographical spaces, yet retain a communal sense of unity. Thus at this point in time the United States which began with a few settlements on the Atlantic seaboard has reached a point where, spanning geographical spaces across land and sea, it includes Alaska and Hawaii in its territorial boundaries.

It should be noted that homes conform both internally and externally to the prevailing styles of interior decoration and architecture. It is hard to imagine a modern family for example moving into a home or apartment failing to purchase paintings, rugs, furniture, mirrors, lamps, kitchen ware, cabinetry and all the other appurtenances that will result in a harmonious and esthetically pleasing space reflecting contemporary styles and usages, and establishing a "home" in the literal and metaphorical sense. On the other hand, it is hard for a Westerner to understand the minimalism that characterized the Japanese home almost to the recent present where "less" is more or to put it conversely "more" is less. Even in Western countries where there is an overall homogeneity of style, and where there has been a rapid exchange of architectural and home decoration ideas, there may still be significant differences that require adjustment on a traveler's part.

If we look at the public buildings, stores, governmental structures that house our legislators, governors, president, police departments, stores and shopping malls, synagogues and churches, public libraries and universities, the variance in style from country to country, and epoch to epoch, becomes even more striking and significant.

It may be added that housing may include variations that contradict our basic expectations. In addition to the conventional structures that shelter family members under one roof, and are often passed down from generation to generation in preserving historical continuity, we must allow for other arrangements such as monasteries and convents where monks and nuns live their lives communally because of common religious convictions—or barracks and ships where soldiers and sailors are brought together because of their commitment to their country's defense.

Semi-socialist communes prospered in part of the nineteenth and twentieth century in the United States as well as the kibbutz in Israel displaying a shared adherence to a particular lifestyle (as do Amish, Shakers, Chasidic, and artistic enclaves), revealing the effects of the collectivistic rather than biological needs.

It may be interesting to contemplate the new conceptual possibilities of a home or shelter once we transcend terrestrial boundaries and traverse the enormous spaces separating us from other planets and galaxies.

ENTERTAINMENT. Much time, money and effort are devoted to our entertainment during our leisure hours involving movies, theaters, concert halls, television, sports, games, etc. Once again it is important to note the enormous differences that exist culturally and historically amongst societies so that a form of entertainment once acceptable may no longer prove so in another time and place. Thus take gladiatorial games in Ancient Rome or the tournaments in Medieval times where the players combatted to the death which are now rejected as inhuman and morally repellent. Similar repugnance is felt today to competitions involving the suffering of animals, bulls, cocks, dogs, etc., that were once tolerated though they may still be practiced in some parts of the world. It is interesting to speculate whether the kinds of violent sports characterizing today's world, like wrestling, boxing, football, hockey, etc., often resulting in massive physical harm will be seen as primitive in their present form to future generations.

In turn, modern times have permitted explicitness and openness in subject matter and language in all forms of entertainment that the past would have considered taboo. It is hard for us to understand the ruckus raised by Flaubert's <u>Madame Bovary</u> or Joyce's <u>Ulysses</u> whose depiction of sexuality now seems tame and a very minor part of their novels' major themes just as our own emphasis on the erotic in practically every artistic realm, television, film, theater, music, etc., would have scandalized our Victorian forbears.

Similar comments can be made about artistic genres and styles that evolved over the ages. Witness the Reality Show on television today that catapults an otherwise ordinary person into public limelight and makes the events of quotidian life the focus of widespread attention—or Rap Music, devoid of all melodious content, that seems all the rage today—both of which would have struck audiences of the past as bizarre and incomprehensible. Thus the short story and novel of modern times took us to newer and deeper levels in understanding human behavior and motivation than the medieval tales of a Chaucer and Boccaccio, however imaginatively and masterfully crafted. Artistic expressions from foreign cultures, Chinese, Indian, Japanese, etc., in music, poetry, drama, and other genres often place an enormous strain on our sensibilities and require considerable adjustment to assimilate and enjoy. It will be interesting to see if future generations similarly provide forms of entertainment that transcend our wildest imaginings and contradict our most basic premises concerning art and amusement.

TOURISM. From the earliest time, men and women have evinced an interest in travel and learning about other people's cultures and customs. If anything this interest has flourished further in today's world fostered through modern modes of transportation that can take us to the remotest parts of the globe in a matter of days. Yet even in Ancient and Medieval times, seemingly insuperable geographical distances did not automatically prove an obstacle and impediment to the touristic urge. Marco Polo's travel to China to encounter foreign cultures and describing this to his fascinated Venetian and European contemporaries testifies to its potency. And to some degree, so do the voyages of the explorers and conquistadores since the time of Columbus to the New World though undertaken for patently commercial, military, and political motives. According to the <u>Canterbury Tales</u>, men and women's urge to travel blossoming in the spring seems instinctual and universal in scope and is intimately linked to our needs for fellowship and social interaction:

> When in April the sweet showers fall
> And pierce the drought of March to the
> root . . .
> And the small fowl are making melody . . .
> Then people long to go on pilgrimages
> And palmers long to seek the stranger
> strands
> Of far-off saints, hallowed in sundry lands

Is it possible that space travel that now has no immediate economic benefit springs not only from our innate desire to explore the universe but also touch base as the alleged sightings of UFO's and science fiction speculations indicate with extra-terrestrial beings, representing a collectivistic need on the part of humanity as a whole for greater cosmological integration and unity?

COSMETOLOGY, JEWELRY, GROOMING. In addition to clothing the market generates enormous activity around bodily ornamentation and adornment, i.e., lipstick, nail polish, manicures, hair styling, perfumes, facial creams, tattooing, etc., emphasizing the standards of beauty prevailing at a particular time and place that from an external perspective may seem bizarre, unnatural and possibly grotesque. Take tattooing for example that was mandated for men in Maori society, regarded as taboo in the Old Testament, and welcome by many as stylish and aesthetic in today's world. The same can be said for hair styling, coming in a myriad of manifestations and changing so radically from generation to generation that nothing is as revelatory as it of a historical period particularly when the coiffure, i.e., Mohawk, Afro, bizarre coloration, etc., represents a 180 degree departure from established practices. Or take as further illustrations of the workings of the collectivistic principle the expensive surgical, dermatological procedures or body-building regimens often sustained with intense physical discomfort and enormous expenditures to achieve conformity to social constructs of beauty that have often little to do with genuine health issues.

WEDDINGS AND FUNERAL RITUALS. It may be appropriate to mention those important climacteric moments that commemorate the different stages of a person's life, birth, coming of age, marriage, death, particularly where they involve people of social stature and celebrity and promote the principle of political and historical continuity. Witness the marriages of Prince Charles and his son Prince William, heirs to the English throne, watched by countless of millions around the globe on television with glued fascination and involving expenditures running no doubt into astronomic proportions. The same is true for funerals and burials, whether personal or political often involving stupendous costs, of which the Pyramids serving as mausoleums for the ancient Pharaohs, securing them a safe voyage to the Next World provide probably the most spectacular and extravagant examples.

HOLIDAYS, which recur with predictable regularity on the calendar, provide the means that strengthen communal bonds. As we have seen, the traditional Thanksgiving turkey dinner serves not a biological but collectivistic need to celebrate our nation's settlement and re-affirm the principles on which it was founded—and, it may be added, becomes for many of us the occasion of mass "pilgrimages" to different parts of the country to reunite us with our families and geographical roots. Christmas too, a lynch pin of our economy with its relentless and prolonged emphasis on the manufacture and sale of commodities, strengthens the bonds uniting us to our families and friends through the ritualized sharing of gifts. New Year's Eve provides a collectivized occasion on practically a global scale with its endless festive celebrations that with the aid of telecommunication seem to occur with near simultaneity. The weekends that sprang originally from the Biblical Sabbath are now an almost universally institutionalized feature of all forms of employment allowing people not only to rest from work but also to indulge in activities, dining, entertainment, traveling, etc., whose value is enriched by being shared with their fellow human beings.

The list can be expanded endlessly. It is impossible to enumerate the seemingly infinite kinds of commodities and services that appear on the market place in response to collectivistic rather than biological needs or, conversely, to list any that are not somehow directly or indirectly involved with them. We strive futilely to draw a distinction between nature and art, between what is innate and instinctual in our psychological makeup, and what is socially acquired and environmentally induced. Commencing with one, we invariably end up with the other.

It may be tempting to draw a distinction between an artistic commodity like a book or a painting and a purely commercial one like an item of furniture or of clothing. The distinction is an ultimately fallacious one. The only genuine distinction is that between "authentic" vs. "inauthentic" commodities—between those that genuinely unite people into a larger collectivity and gratify their collectivistic needs and those that do not.

Ultimately an authentic commodity is rooted in the imagination, an inauthentic one is not. Thus an artistic commodity like the kind of painting favored in Communist countries promoting its ideological propaganda, or an anti-Semitic book produced in Nazi Germany, although ostensibly classified as art and even displaying a high degree of technical skill, is no more authentic than a product that caters to the lowest of instincts, say, pornography, in its quest of purely commercial success. On the other hand, an apparel by a master tailor, or a piece of furniture produced by a skilled craftsman, or culinary innovations by a dedicated chef can provide a profoundly authentic and moving experience whereby collectivistic needs are truly gratified.

If we stray from this ideal, it is that other factors may be involved—the seductiveness of false advertisement which may persuade us that we want things when we don't—the emphasis of an economy driven by mass production on sheer volume as a self-authenticating principle prioritizing quantity above quality—"the keeping up with the Jones" mentality, resulting in competition rather than social cohesion—all of which diminish and undermine rather than promote the collectivistic principle on which genuine market interaction is based.

It is obvious that certain historical periods, social contexts or geographical locations may be more conducive to the inner workings of the imaginative processes than others. Perhaps the following story by Collier, "Witch's Money," already mentioned in our introduction will bring out this point. A painter in his travels in Basque country encounters a town far away from the well-trodden path, and is smitten by the scenery. He buys a house, confident that he will able to paint in this stimulating setting. However the xenophobic natives far removed from the rest of the world are deeply suspicious of him and regard his strange use of language punctuated by wild tropes and extravagant figures of speech with amazement as if he were an alien from a remote planet. They notice that he uses checks to defray the purchase of a house, something they have never encountered before, and then when these are successfully cashed, mistakenly assume that the checks represent actual cash and that since he has a book of them he must be extremely wealthy.

One night, they conspire to kill him and steal the checks which are divided equally—perhaps the first expression of the collectivistic principle albeit it in a sinister form. The effect on the economy is as quick as it is transformative. Within a matter of a few weeks the village which economically had been stagnant is abuzz with ever-accelerating economic activity. Property exchanges hands at a rapid rate. Credit is generously extended. Women are able to provide dowries and get married. What in fact is most noteworthy is that the townspeople begin making what is the equivalent of capital improvement and undertaking entrepreneurial risks as they replace the village's mule track to the main highway with a regular road whose commercial traffic will provide it greater accessibility to potential customers and start purchasing materials that will improve the quality and quantity of their produce.

While the townspeople will eventually be disabused of their illusions, the point is clear: That what drives the economy is not the actuality of things but our perceptions of them. That Art and the Artist stand not at the margins of the commercial world but at its center. And of course that ultimately the real cause of wealth is the collectivistic spirit uniting the marketplace into a truly cohesive whole. What the checks awaken is something that was always there in latent form but needed a catalyst in the artist's arrival to bring about its external manifestation.

If commodities satisfy both biological and collectivistic needs, it is necessary to mention a third need that divides people and impels them to achieve a sense of domination and superiority rather than of community in their economic relations. Let us take food again as our first example. Obviously, there is a limit to how much food one can absorb at a time unless we think of the absolutely repellent practice in Ancient Rome where the rich would disgorge themselves to consume more. But observe one can have the rarest foods brought from around the world—one can eat in palatial surroundings from plates of gold and silver—one can employ servants to cater to and gratify one's every eating need and habit—one can use the most experienced and skillful of chefs in creation of exquisitely tasty and imaginative cuisines—so that one can consume a meal quantitatively circumscribed within biological limits but qualitatively representing hundreds, or even thousands, of meals in terms of expenditure compared to those eaten by people less fortunate in this regard.

The same could be said of clothing or housing—the manorial estates that span thousands of acres and are adorned with the most expensive furniture and art work—or the rare jewels, furs and exquisitely crafted tailoring involving materials garnered from every part of the globe—that represent expenditures unimaginably larger than those spent by the average consumer.

While these sums could involve genuine material comforts and esthetic pleasures, it cannot be doubted that they also spring in many cases from an anti-collectivistic need to be superior to and different from those who cannot afford them and that the pleasure from owning and using them arises essentially from the fact that others do not.

Yet even here it must be pointed out that such lavish meals, stunning apparel and extravagant surroundings must again be shared with others of the same moneyed and privileged class without which they would not be truly enjoyable.

Take the aristocrats of Medieval times in their castles surrounded by the shacks of the peasantry, or the Southern plantation owners who could command their slaves to do their every bidding, or the industrial captains of the nineteenth century in their palatial mansions dominating their factory workers, yet needing other aristocrats, plantation owners and magnates with and through whom they could achieve genuine collectivistic ties, and without whom they would be condemned to an isolated and meaningless existence despite all their extravagant displays of wealth.

It may be useful to look at the area of consumption in our own country in terms of a specific group effectively barred from it, i.e., the Afro Americans who were brought against their will from Africa to America to till the cotton fields and enabled the accumulation of tremendous wealth of the plantation owners: On the one hand, they were torn from the cultural contexts that gave them a sense of collectivized identification and nurture. On the other hand, they were completely excluded from genuine meaningful participation in the market made possible through their arduous labor. This was true even after the Civil War despite the appropriate Constitutional amendments freeing them from slavery: Witness the Jim Crow laws which barred them from restaurants, hotels, schools, and other places only whites were permitted into. What purpose from a pragmatic or utilitarian purpose did this exclusion serve? How could this be explained in terms of Adam Smith's principle of self interest? Would not the restaurants, hotels, theaters, schools, etc., that barred them have profited from the added income

Black patronage would have conferred? Rather the economic exclusion which did not necessarily benefit the whites monetarily, and in fact in many cases may have disadvantaged them by depriving them of possible sources of revenue, originated out of the sense of superiority and dominancy it conferred.

It was only (to give but one example of historical change) when a boycott of a segregated bus transportation system in Montgomery was successfully organized under the leadership of Dr. King and when the utilitarian needs of the bus company were pitted against the anti-collectivistic ones of the community to the point where they exacted an unbearable financial toll that a reprioritization of needs and objectives underpinning economic conduct was rethought and reformulated.

The same has been true for every other form of discrimination whether it be in the form of religious bigotry, sexism, caste system, etc. The Jew for example who in the Middle Ages and tragically under the Nazi occupation could not live in the same neighborhoods as a Christian; the Indian pariah who was not allowed to contaminate the presence of the higher castes with his own; women who for a long time were barred from the advantages of genuine economic participation—the list is endless, so endless that it could almost be thought that the dominative instinct is the only one characterizing economic relations to the exclusion of all cooperation and collectivization.

It must therefore be concluded that a marketplace can exist only where commodities are shared. The communal feast involves by definition "community." As the word "company" indicates, company exists where bread ("panis") is shared. There will be historical inequalities of course as noted between men and women, Blacks and whites, employer and employee, etc. If the marketplace endures at all under these circumstances it is because the elite form a system of inclusion and community amongst themselves. However, if the inequalities reach a point where the collectivistic needs are frustrated, as the members at the top of the pyramid begin to compete with one another in turn, and create ever tighter and narrower hierarchies, the marketplace will be atomized, dismembered and fragmented and prevented from fulfilling its function to weld us into a larger coherent communal unity where our economic objectives are pursued in collaboration with others rather than in antagonism to them.

❧ CHAPTER III ❧

Work: The Concept of Role

Having focused on consumption the next step in our economic analysis is to turn to the concept of work. Like consumption, it is driven by utilitarian motives as well as collectivistic ones. On the one hand, Smith's baker, butcher and brewer need to work to fulfill their basic instinctual and biological needs and in turn be able to purchase the commodities on which their well-being and survival depend. But in addition they and all other participants in the market place need to work together in a larger social economic setting not only as a means but also as an end in and for itself. A Robinson Crusoe to the extent that such a phenomenon is conceivable may work to satisfy his biological needs, but it is only as he comes into contact with another human being,

Friday, that the collectivistic dimension of work comes into play.

Let us look at the actor as an example of the collectivistic dimension and definition of work. It is obvious that in familiarizing himself with his particular role he must of course do so in conjunction with other actors to achieve the dramatic effect the play for which he has been chosen is intended to convey. Some roles may of course be more important than others. It is obvious to take <u>Hamlet</u> as an example that not every actor in the cast is capable of playing the star role. Exceptional interpretive and artistic skills that may require years of experience and practice are indispensible in this regard. But still to the degree that the play succeeds at all this depends on the interaction of all the actor participants, major or minor, to integrate their efforts into a seamless cohesive whole.

If we pursue the matter further, the actor's role must mesh with an even wider interconnected network of roles for the theatrical production to succeed, including:

* The author who has written the play— which in the case of a Shakespeare shows the historical continuity of a marketplace

that spans centuries and even, if we add a
Sophocles and Aeschylus, millennia

* The schools where the actor has received his
  training particularly when he has to perform
  Repertoire Theater as mentioned above

* The theater owner who has supplied the
  setting where the play can be performed in a
  comfortable and effective manner

* The stage designers and setters who since the
  nineteenth century have become increasingly
  involved with the appropriate clothing the
  actors wear and stage furniture arrangements
  suitable to the particular place and period
  the play represents

* The newspaper notifications that provide
  information of the theatrical event

* The restaurants where the audience is
  likely to have their meal before or after the
  performances and the transportation system
  that enables them to get to the theater district
  that have become a necessary ancillary of the
  theatrical event

     * The post-theater parties and the Emmy and Oscar celebrations that commemorate excellence of performance that have become a ritualistic part of the entertainment business

If we add today's movie and television industries, an even more complex and diverse array of factors and of technological skills enters into the economic calculations.

What is true of the acting world is true of course for other areas of economic endeavor as well. To give but a limited set of examples:

     * The academy where a faculty must be united to fashion a set of meaningful curriculum, admission and graduation requirements, and provide research facilities upon which progress and advancement in every area of modern life depend

     * The corporations that must be meaningfully united in their vast and complex organization to provide the effective manufacture and sale of the product(s) for which they are designed

* The athletic teams whose players must harmonize effectively if they are to win against their opponents, the instruments and uniforms they need to play the games, their lengthy amount of training sometimes lasting for years to obtain the skills they acquire, the arenas where they play, and in modern times the media necessary to broadcast their athletic performances to the public and the advertisements that make this possible

* The shopping malls and department stores which carry a wide array of products that must be effectively integrated to provide an authentic shopping experience

* The hospitals that must integrate a wide set of services and skills that provide necessary health care to patients sick with every conceivable illness

* The newspaper and magazine industries that furnish their readers with important information about current events and issues involving their environment on a local, national and international level

If we wish, the entire marketplace in its vast variety and complexity represents a skein of interconnectedness where every economic activity coheres with every other and cannot be viewed in isolation.

Hence the tragedy of unemployment which not only deprives the individual full access to the commodities he would like to enjoy but also deprives him of a sense of dignity and satisfaction work confers.

It may be interesting to turn at this juncture to Robinson's poem, "The Mill," which describes effectively the psychological wound and harm of unemployment. In the poem, the miller who has earned his living because of the mill is now out of work as a result of the new technology which has rendered mills useless and obsolete. Although the same fate has affected thousands of other millers—as technological change always cuts a wide swath of victimization—the poem achieves a profound subjective effect which allows the reader identification with the miller always referred to anonymously and in the third person. Outwardly it does not seem that he is affected on the obvious economic level—i.e., in terms of eating and shelter. Thus the poem begins with his wife having prepared an afternoon tea—one of life's little luxuries and non-necessities.

When he is conspicuously absent from the meal, she is disturbed by his having uttered the enigmatic sentence "There are no millers any more" (otherwise having given no hint of his despair), and upon further enquiry finds out he has killed himself, his body hanging from a raft in the mill achieving an identification with the means of production to which his life is consecrated. Unable to sustain the loss and her own subsequent deprivation of a meaningful spousal role—as his life is defined by the mill, hers is by her husband—she drowns herself as both disappear from the social setting where they no longer have any significant impact, leaving no trace of their existence or in fact of their having existed at all. Instead of economic motives per se, the devastation of losing a role that provides the individual with a social identity and fills his or her days with meaningful activity seems more than the two can bear, made worse by society's indifference and in fact obliviousness as to what is taking place.

In a sense the collectivistic spirit that manifests itself in work follows integrally from that displayed in consumption. Obviously, behind every meaningful and authentic commodity that succeeds in integrating society and binding its members into a larger whole there must be someone who has produced it in conjunction with others. Just as we cannot meaningfully draw a hierarchization among different kinds of commodities—they either spring from the imagination or not—neither can we draw a distinction among different kinds of work. They too involve the imaginative process. Hence the concept of the "poet" implied a "maker" in the original Greek word from which it is etymologically derived. Either the maker complies with the genuine forces of inspiration and imaginative processes or defies, modifies and compromises them to where he does not produce a commodity genuinely fulfilling the collectivistic urge but instead fabricates a simulacrum or illusion of one, a "magician" as it were who relies on the power of unconscious suggestion and persuasion as opposed to an artist who challenges our ordinary perceptions and transcends the limitations by which these are circumscribed.

The sense of creativity is reflected not only in works of art as classically defined, books, paintings, architecture, music, sculpture, etc., but in many other economic activities, say, tailoring, dining, interior decoration, so forth and so on. As previously noted, talent and creativity are not equally allocated and distributed. Not everyone can be a Shakespeare, Cervantes, Michelangelo, Da Vinci, Beethoven, etc., or to widen the scope of our subject matter not everyone can be a Chippendale, Coco Channel, an Escoffier, who revolutionizes the concept of apparel, interior decoration, or eating habits for millions of men and women. Obviously such superiority of talent deserves commendation and reward. In honoring these people and their contributions to humanity, we commemorate and reward ourselves and strengthen the collectivistic bonds that bind us. But the myth of "greatness" so rampant in the nineteenth century can be pushed too far, and can be used as an excuse by society to discourage creativity and originality or serve as cop-outs for people who do not rise to the challenges that will enrich their lives.

Again, we can draw attention to the story "Witch's Money" as illustrating the premises upon which a genuine marketplace is based. The painter who arrives in the Basque village is a "worker" in the true collectivist sense of the word: He creates commodities that will not necessarily gratify the biological needs of others such as food, housing, clothing (though as noted these often possess profound collectivistic dimensions) but their need to belong to a larger communal whole where their individual identities are enhanced, transcended, enriched and fulfilled. At first, the artist, an adventurous spirit who has traveled the world, who responds spontaneously to his environment and intuitive perceptions, and who sees opportunities where others do not, mystifies and frightens the townspeople as if he were a being from another universe. Yet as soon as he moves into the village and purchases a permanent dwelling place where he can practice his art, and begins to communicate with them in extravagant tropes and metaphors that transcend and defy their conventional use of language, he does exercise an enriching effect on some of their lives:

> There was no doubt about it, there was something very magnificent about this madman . . . . "To listen," said little Guis, "is to be drunk without spending a penny. You think you understand; you seem to fly through the air."
>
> "I somehow had the delectable impression that I was rich," said Arago.

By contrast, the townspeople represent a state of alienation in its starkest terms, pushing the antimonies of literalness and imagination, isolation and connectivity to their extreme form, and setting the stage for the dramatic impact of the artist's arrival. After his death, sustained by the checks he has bequeathed to them, they begin to undertake "work" in the true sense of the word as a source not only of physical necessity but also of inner fulfillment. There is no limit to what their organized and collectivistic efforts can achieve as they reach out first to one another and then to the wider world beyond, transforming a barren into a fruitful economy—"the village blossomed like an orchid sprung from a dry stick"—filling their lives with unwonted energy, enthusiasm, and purpose. If the ending of the story eventually spells out their doom as they enter the bank in Perpignan to cash their checks, it is only because like many individuals and societies they mistake the symbolic dimensions of money for a literal one, and fail to fully assimilate the truth that the collectivistic principle is the only genuine source of wealth.

To conclude our analysis of the subject, if the impetus for work comes from a collectivistic need it can also involve an anti-collectivistic one as reflected in the quest for power, domination, and superiority. The most obvious and egregious examples of such domination include the lot of the peasantry in the Middle Ages and in post-feudal times, slaves abducted from Africa to toil in the plantations of the South in its cotton and tobacco fields. The plight of the serfs and slaves resulted in the enormous accumulation of wealth and material comfort for their masters as exemplified in their castles and plantation houses, their vast acreages of land, and other accouterments of wealth and power. In short, their oppression represented a callous and brutally exploitative endeavor to enhance one's wealth at the expense of others, pushing the principle of self-interest to its ultimate limit. But what has to be equally stressed and is inextricably intertwined with this is the sense of superiority that cannot be totally explained in terms of utilitarian objectives which cast feudal lords and the slaveholders of the ante-bellum South into the role of a higher and different species of human beings whose destiny it was they believed to dominate and master others.

As Countee Cullen expressed so pithily in relation to a latter-day exemplification of this mentality: "She even thinks that up heaven/Her class lies late and snores/While black cherubs rise at seven/To do celestial chores."

Did the sense of racial or social superiority result in or from the denigration of the peasants or Blacks in the marketplace? Which was cause and effect? Did the fact that feudal lords or white slaveholders thought of the peasantry or of Blacks as inferior result in their elimination from their rightful place in the workplace? Or did the exclusion from a genuine role in the work place result in a perception of them as a lower class of beings? Or did the two reinforce each other as inseparable components of a larger cycle? While it is impossible to formulate the cause-effect relation with precision, the conclusion is the same: The fragmentation of the market place rather than its cohesion and unification.

The nineteenth century when theoretically more liberal and democratic tendencies prevailed which saw the emergence of factories and the institution of the assembly line also saw the emergence of a new economic force: Labor. This referred to the masses of unskilled people, the "proletariat" to use another term, who were free to move to areas where work was located, and who were needed to operate the factories, mines, transportation systems, etc., characterizing modern industry. While their lot was not of the same ilk as that of the peasantry or of the slaves, they had no say over the conditions of their work. They exhibited no sign of the collectivistic principle characterizing work in the authentic sense of the word in relation to other workers or their employers. Unlike the actor role that shows autonomy and self-expression, they became a kind of puppet whose every movement and gesture were dictated to the last degree by their employers, denied all opportunity of individualism and spontaneity. Their lot could be rationalized and justified by the principle of hierarchy that demanded compliancy to authority and suppression of individuality as the only conceivable basis of genuine economic growth and development dictated by the imperatives of mass production and industrial technology. Whatever the validity of this perspective, such hierarchized work arrangements sprang not only from the employers' quest of enormous economic rewards and advantages but also for mastery and domination as an objective in and of itself, seeing themselves in the manner of feudal lords and plantation owners as a different species of humanity with regard to the working, i.e., "lower," classes.

Another example that will shed light on this subject is furnished by the Afro-Americans who were freed from the trammels of slavery after the Civil War, but in reality were kept in a state of economic vassalage where the opportunities to participate in the market place in a meaningful way were denied. Thus, the biography of Malcolm X reveals that he once expressed a desire as a student to his teacher to become a lawyer and that the teacher's answer was that he lower his sights and try to obtain something more reasonable and pragmatical. Was the teacher a racist who felt Blacks should be kept in their place—or was he sincerely realistic in his assessment of what was and what was not achievable under the conditions prevailing at the time? Whatever his motives, the attitude reflected the anti-collectivistic tendencies of the whites who wanted to exclude Blacks from the collective market place not from a purely utilitarian self-serving perspective—after all the talents of a Malcolm X would have benefitted whites as well as Blacks and could hardly prove a source of disadvantage—but from a desire to exclude and keep Blacks in their place, bolstering the whites' sense of superiority as a self-validating objective.

In short, it was propelled and fueled by the same motivation already noted evinced by whites to exclude Blacks from theaters, restaurants, middle class neighborhoods and housing, and other areas of consumption as a necessary tactic to achieve and nurture a sense of superiority and dominance.

Still further examples can be found in the case of women who were confined to stereotypic roles and functions and excluded from full participation in major areas of employment until very recently, and whose exclusion still has not been satisfactorily resolved. How could this exclusion be justified if utilitarian objectives provide the only meaningful gauge in terms of which economic activity should be measured? Would not cooperation of the sexes in the economic sphere have worked to their mutual advantage? And in fact could any economy in the present and future continue effectively without the contribution of women? In short, the same kind of quest for superiority manifested in the relation between the lord and the serf, the plantation owner and the slave, Black and white, has also manifested itself in that between the sexes.

Further examples can be found in terms of sexual orientation, age, religion, social standing, and all the other arbitrary factors that have been used to legitimize economic fragmentation and exclusion. Witness the brutal elimination of Jews from the work place under the Nazi regime where they had previously made such prodigious contributions to science, art, literature, technology and every area of commerce or the restriction of the outcasts of India to the lowest and most menial occupations regardless of individual talent or intellectual aptitude. Once again as in the case of consumption, the list of examples of exclusionism in the work place is endless.

The collectivistic principle cannot be found in its pure form in any society and may in fact be countered and negated by the anti-collectivistic principle that shatters and fragments such economic communalization. The two tendencies have coexisted throughout history. Thus if feudal lords, white plantation owners, and the captains of industry dominated and exerted power over serfs, Blacks, and factory workers, to the extent that they cooperated with one another, the concept of a genuine market place revealing collectivistic tendencies was partially retained. But where the anti-collectivistic tendency overpowers the collectivistic tendency, as eventually it must unless creative forms of revitalization such as the Civil Rights movement, unionization, social legislation, women's movement, etc., emerge as a way of restoring it, the marketplace in the genuine sense of the word declines and disintegrates and no longer fulfills the function for which it was intended, resulting in a void where human beings cannot satisfy their fundamental needs whether physically or communally by meaningful participation in it.

❧ CHAPTER IV ❧

Trade: Buying and Selling

In this chapter, the collectivistic principle will be applied to the phenomenon of trade. When consumption and production were analyzed, we focused on the individual consumer and worker in relation to others through the concept of commodity and role. Now our focus will be directed to the two parties, the seller and the buyer, who are connected with one another in the transactional negotiation to the degree to which they can be disentangled from the web of socio-economic relations with millions, and in fact even tens and hundreds of millions, of other consumers and laborers to whom they are integrally connected.

Does the relation between the two correspond to individualistic or collectivistic needs? Does the buyer come to the market with specific needs for food, clothing, shelter, medicine, etc., which must be satisfied in his search for physical and individual well being? And does the seller come to the market with the need to sell his good and services to obtain the money which will permit him to buy the commodities he needs in turn?

In other words, do the buyer and seller see in one another a means and only a means to a purely personal end? Or do both come to the market seeing the exchange of goods and services as an activity that is gratifying in and of itself and cannot be separated from the context in which it is embedded?

This might seem like a strange and eccentric view of the market place, but is it if examined further and especially given Smith's view that commerce involves man's disposition to truck, barter and exchange? Let us look at trade first from the point of view of the seller whatever the product or service he is marketing may be. Is there a point where the seller, say, a Rockefeller or Vanderbilt, a Jobs or Gates, just to mention names that ring a bell, has accumulated so much money that he finally can desist from further activity and enjoy the fruits of his labors for the rest of his life time and even that of his progeny for generations to come? Or is it rather more likely that the process of creating products and negotiating their sale is so vitally challenging and stimulating that it must be pursued as long as possible as an end in and of itself?

The same is true of the shopper. Is there a point where the shopper having reached his or her limit will no longer engage in the shopping activity? Is it not possible that as a result of going to the market place where commodities are traded he or she may find something so totally and unexpectedly stimulating and captivating that he will not be able to resist the temptation to purchase it? To be more specific, can the art connoisseur, the gem collector, the theatergoer, the avid book reader, the world traveler whose destination is not only strange and exotic places but also the marketplaces associated with them ever be truly satisfied in terms of the gratifications these activities entail?

True, work and shopping may be extended to a point where these are not psychologically healthful and where they become addictive and obsessive, possibly even pathological, and constitute an impediment to personal fulfillment and the pursuit of other areas of life entailing friendship, family relations, leisure, relaxation, etc., in the sense that any activity and pursuit when extended beyond its psychologically salubrious limits becomes destructive and pathological. But that does not prevent them from having a meaningful and significant role in our lives in the context of the market place when utilized in moderation and restraint.

If we look at the market place as a place where people trade whether it be the colorful stalls filled with all kinds of produce associated with countries like India an Mexico or with the exciting shopping areas of cities like Paris and New York, or auction houses whose sales are often electrifying and constitute the grist for news stories, or street fairs and bazaars which still retain the colorful interaction of primitive bazaars, or the market place in its entirety that reaches global dimensions and cannot be structured, explored and accessed without the aid of advertisements or Google-provided information, it assumes a creature-like being larger than its constituent parts, nourishing them as it is nourished by them in turn.

In this connection, the example of "Witch's Money" may again prove useful and instructive. After the artist buys his house from Foiral, and when the villagers get his checkbook, trade begins to flourish at first slowly and afterwards with ever-accelerating speed. The first character to do so is a Barilles who has an eye on his neighbor Arago's orchard, and initializes the negotiation when he visits the latter at his home.

At first, Barilles is extremely circumspect and cautious about expressing an interest in the orchard that might affect the asking price—as is Arago from his end in selling it. Then gradually as they skirt the issue and as their conversation passes through typical phases of "civility, sarcasm, rage, fury and desperation," they strike a deal at 20,000 francs leading to their mutual satisfaction. This becomes the occasion of social jubilation and has profound consequences for the community as a whole. Everyone was delighted, the author tells us, by the sale: it was felt things were beginning to "move" in the village. This is soon followed by further transactions involving other participants and an ever wider range of commodities and services that would have been previously unimaginable: Vigne's sale of his mules to Ques for eight thousand francs—Lloube's of his cork concession to Foiral for fifteen thousand—Madame Arago's brass collection for sixty five. Then further fanciful and imaginative developments ensue that enhance the town's economy and strengthen its collective bonds: Barilles calling his little shop "Grand Café Glacier de l'Universe et des Pyrenees"—Lloubes returning from Perpignan with a "bale of ladies' clothing, designed . . . by the very devil himself"—the widow Loyau offering room, board and clothing to some unattached ladies and giving select parties in the evening. Everyone seeks to get into the act drawn by the market's magnetic force as well as by the actual desirability and need of the commodities involved. Activity begets energy which in turn begets further activity, so forth and so on, and the town marked by xenophobic isolation and determined resistance to change now becomes a "marketplace" in the genuine sense of the word without there being a limit to its expansion as long as the townspeople remain true to the collectivistic impulses causing its emergence.

The second question to answer in analyzing the marketplace is: What is the price that a commodity sells or should sell for? This has been the subject of economics as well as ethics from time immemorial. What is the process whereby the seller and buyer arrive at a price in terms of which an exchange of goods, services, wares and commodities takes place? Is it motivated by purely individualistic needs? Do we as sellers want to get as much as possible for the produce we merchandise or as shoppers do we seek to pay as little as possible? Or is there a collectivist process (which paradoxically the village's conspiratorial group seems able to achieve) where we neither overreach or are overreached and feel we have made a fair deal that is of satisfaction to both of us and which constitutes a firm basis for future negotiations?

History provides us with endless examples where the price set on a commodity and service is simply not a realistic reflection of its value but represents a gross distortion and falsification thereof.

Was this not the case in pre-Civil War South when the slave was dragged from African shores to work beneath the scorching sun and continuous threat of the lash to provide the white plantation owner with all the accouterments of wealth and power?

Was this not the case where the wages which the proletariat working in the factories of the Industrial Revolution earned were a distortion of the real value of their labor?

Is this not also the basis of the argument of feminists who assert the value of women's work in the market place is still not reflected even today in the price that it commands?

The same can be said of children who have been exploited over the centuries and are still being exploited in many parts of the globe—or workers in Third World countries who cannot hold their own in their negotiations with the more advantaged economies of the West—or monopolies that allow a small number of people to obtain such exclusive control over products and services that they can dictate whatever prices they see fit.

If language throughout history can be and has been used to distort the truth of things as they really are, there is no reason why in the economic realm price, a form of symbolic representation, cannot be used in the same deceptive and unjust manner.

However, the point to make here is that to the degree that a marketplace can function at all, however flawed at different times and places, it does—it must—on some level reflect a meaningful interaction between seller and buyer based on principles of integrity and truth, involving a price that is fair and satisfactory to both.

Thus as previously stated if the plantation or factory owners exploited their slaves and workers, they themselves must have been involved in fair and egalitarian transactions with one another if the collectivistic principle gratifying both and permitting the market place to continue can be fulfilled.

However, if the anti-collectivistic forces pitting trader against trader in conflict rather than mutual cooperation extend to the point where a smaller and smaller number of people exert power, then the market place in any authentic sense of the word will cease to exist and collapse as may have happened innumerable time in history and that could happen now if greater and greater numbers of people feel increasingly alienated from a marketplace that can no longer supply them with the nurture necessary to their physical and communal needs

❧ Chapter V ❧

The Decline and Fall of Markets

1. The Role of Currency and Government

It may be worthwhile to examine the birth and death of markets, and to consider them organisms similar to human beings who are born, age, sicken and die though markets are sometimes capable of regeneration. Markets are never static. The bonds that hold them together strengthen and weaken, expand and contract. This happened during the Great Depression in the 1930's in the United States when employment, trade and consumption as well as credit availability necessary to business reflected a devastating weakening of the collectivistic principle.

At the heart of the financial community as in any community is the element of credibility and credulity. If, as in the story "Witch's Money," A gives B money or a check equivalent to money, B's assumption is that such money or check will be accepted in turn by a third person C, so that A, B, and C are joined in a mutually beneficial union. If B does not have the confidence that the money he gets from A will enable him to buy the commodities and services he wants, this when spread over a large number of people participating in the market will have a debilitative effect on financial negotiations and transactions. The economic "stream" will be choked and impeded, freeze and congeal, inhibiting movement, flow, i.e., "currency," its defining characteristic.

Without credibility and shared confidence, human beings will not enter into interactions connecting them in trade, consumption, or work, but remain apart and isolated, ungratified in terms of their biological or collectivistic needs.

This is true even in cases where transactions are carried on in gold. Thus the introduction of paper currency in Europe occurred when Marco Polo brought it on his return from China. The Venetians were at first suspicious and skeptical of the new means of exchange, as the villagers were at first suspicious of the checks the artist owned and used, but eventually adjusted, and found that a market based on it operated far more efficiently than on the cumbersome exchange of gold. Still gold, or rather the belief in gold, remains at the bottom of our economy in today's sophisticated world. But remember that even with gold however valuable and universally desired the element of trust and imagination is at work. If a person sells the services or commodities he has produced for gold bullion but finds that because of inflation or other reasons the gold he received will not enable him to meet his needs and wants, he will of course feel shortchanged, frustrated, disinclined to pursue his market activities. Multiply this by a multitude of people in the same predicament and the effects on the marketplace will be ruinous. There is no sure reality that one can hold on to except the collectivistic premise as the basis of economic growth and interaction as the Midases and Silas Marners of this world have discovered to their despair.

Even the simplest system where money is not used, i.e., a barter system (to the degree it can be called a system), necessitates mutual confidence to function effectively.

Thus in the story "Witch's Money" the epiphany which reveals how an economy really works will occur when the villagers go to the bank of the nearby town of Perpignan and realize that the checks they have traded with cannot be redeemed for French francs. No doubt poetic justice will mete out their individual punishments as proceedings are instituted to determine the how's and why's involved in the checks and their procurement so that the sardonic laugh with which the story ends will be on them, not the artist. But what is more important, the whole economy of the village involving genuine collectivistic interaction, enormous release of energy, and the generation of productive wealth will regress to its former impecunious self, possibly even further. The village may die somewhat after the manner of ghost towns dotting the American West where lively trade and commerce once took place. The only way "out" is through the realization that it is not the checks themselves or the francs or even gold they thought they could redeem them for but the collectivistic premise to work with one another that brought them their begotten wealth.

It is of course true that in some cases, say, as in the Great Depression government intervention may prove helpful. It is difficult to see how the American marketplace or any marketplace past or present anywhere in the world can survive without it. Again, with reference to the story "Witch's Money," it is significant to note that the first important transaction in the village as far removed from the centers of governmental and political institutions as possible involves the participation of a larger social and apparently legal framework: "The witnesses were called in; Barilles handed over one of his *billets*, and received five thousand in cash from the box Arago kept in his chimney. Everyone was delighted by the sale."

The concepts of "government" and "market" are not mutually exclusive. Government is inextricably bound with the market place, and the distinction between the two driven by political rather than economic imperatives is arbitrary and fallacious. To function effectively, government must reflect the collectivistic spirit where men and women work for the common good and overcome their private interests and factionalism. Government is an instrument through which the collectivistic premise achieves its ends—not a substitute for it. Where this collectivistic premise is impeded by anti-collectivist forces and impeded moreover by anti-collectivistic forces of such an extent that any degree at collectivization is unachievable, its intervention is valueless and counterproductive.

2. Markets in Transformation: Rome and Christianity

In accordance with the economic postulates of this book, the marketplace should gratify both the collectivistic as well as the biological needs of the individuals involved in it. Sometimes this occurs, sometimes not. While the marketplace can weather anti-collectivistic forces, there is a point where it cannot and declines as it fails to fulfill its role and function.

A relevant historical example may be found in Ancient Rome, which through its mighty military apparatus unparalleled in history and strong belief in its Manifest Destiny was able to dominate and conquer the rest of the then known civilized world and enjoy a totally disproportionate share of its wealth. The distinction between citizen and non-citizen is a perfect example of as rigid a class structure (to use modern nomenclature) as can be imagined.

Rebellion and resistance proved futile as exemplified in the failed attempts of the ancient Jews to free themselves from the Roman yoke, which led only to the destruction of the Temple, the razing of Jerusalem, and the Jewish Diaspora.

Christianity, originating in Judea, supplied another solution, apolitical and non-military, that successfully spread throughout the remotest parts of the Roman Empire and consisted essentially of a belief in life in the Next World, a spiritual "marketplace," as it were, where human beings' needs would be collectively gratified regardless of origin under the governance of Christ and in the company of fellow Christian believers.

The theological premises on which Christianity rested were not formulated all at once, but evolved over centuries to crystallize in a finalized fixed form, and in a way that would allow it to perform its redemptive mission in a credible and convincing manner.

Without going into detail and summarizing the necessary elements, these consisted of: The divine nature of Jesus seen as the Son of God and on a equal basis with Him; the concept of Original Sin, the result of the Fall, which prevented human beings from acting as free agents exercising their free will and necessitating Christ's crucifixion; the spiritual aspect of human beings that survived after death and required the renunciation of the materialistic riches and benefits furnished by the markets in the "here" and "now"; and the establishment of the Church as the mystical body of

Christ manifesting his presence in perpetuity or at least until the Second Coming.

The concept spread through the Roman Empire and its constituencies that no longer regarded themselves as self-contained and separate but parts of a larger whole, united in their common subjugation by the Romans and common hunger for liberation.

"Give unto Caesar what is Caesar"—with this motto the original Evangelists attempted to avoid a direct confrontation with Roman rule which could only result in their defeat.

In short, the Christian religion came as a response to the historical phenomenon of the Roman Empire and the deep traumatic hurt this engendered amongst the conquered to their sense of self-worth and dignity.

It may be interesting to note that the Christian concept of the Savior was linked historically with the Jewish concept of the Messiah whereby a leader, the anointed one, would establish peace amongst nations and witness the return of Jews to their homeland. The concept of the Messiah was however not a historical but post-historical phenomenon and was not intended to spur consequences for the immediate present so that if a historical figure did appear who proclaimed himself as such, and succeeded moreover in inspiring a sizeable following, this had profoundly tragic consequences.

For the Christians, the Messiah (i.e., Christ) was an actual being, divine and human, living in a particular place and at a particular time, who brought liberation and salvation to the world with the assurance that those who accepted him and his precepts would find a place in the Next World, the Kingdom of God, and thereby be able to satisfy the collectivistic needs frustrated in this world.

The Christian religion which originated with the early Jewish Christians, who felt compelled to share their faith with others, spread to the rest of the Roman Empire and found resonance with its non-Jewish inhabitants, the Gentiles, who similarly sought liberation from Roman rule and oppression.

As the Gospel spread, Christianity had at once a transformative effect on the Roman world and in turn was transformed by it. The Evangelists who sought to universalize the Christian gospel severed the connection between religion and ethnic identity by rejecting the Mosaic code. Obviously, the spread of Christianity would not have succeeded had the Evangelists clung to the parochialisms of the Old Testament, i.e., male circumcision, dietary inhibitions, the observance of the Sabbath, the exclusive religious significance of Jerusalem and its Temple, the numerous holidays marking the Jewish calendar, etc., all of which had meaning for the Jews but were foreign and onerous to the Gentiles, who had no wish to exchange one form of domination for another. What was sought was something truly universal, i.e., "catholic," free of all indigenous and native alloys impeding its success and collectivizing as many disparate adherents in the Empire as possible.

The phenomenon of martyrdom so central to the mythology and history of the early church is another factor that must be looked at in this context. Although Jesus' advocacy of the principle of giving unto Caesar what is Caesar's, to God what is God's, shielded the early Christians against reprisals, theological doctrines eventually do have institutional effects and political repercussions. This happened under the imperial rule of Diocletian when the Christians who had grown in numbers and constituted a sizeable constituency, i.e., were no longer an insignificant minority, refused to accede to the imperial edict to worship the official gods on whom the welfare of Rome depended, proving a genuine socio-political threat that had to be dealt with and punished. But the Christian religion had developed to such a wide extent that it was longer possible to reverse or contain its course. More importantly, death constituted no threat—the Christian was convinced that he or she would be resurrected in the Next World and in fact welcomed his/her martyrdom as ensuring it. Death not only lost its terror. It gained a certain allure and demonstrated as in many ideological, political, religious situations that the collectivistic premise trumps the imperatives of biological and individualistic needs so that persecution ironically abetted the very ideology it sought to crush.

The saying "What profiteth a man if he gain the world but lose his soul in the process?" could not have been more effectively illustrated.

Eventually, even citizens of Rome who had previously enjoyed all the prerogatives of imperial power joined the growing Christian community in order to gratify their collectivistic needs, finalizing the arc swinging from Palestine to Rome and reversing the one the Romans pursued in their conquests to the utmost outposts of the known world. The transformation of the Empire into a Christian community was completed. This integration of the antithesis of Roman vs. non-Roman in terms of a new synthesis, Christian, endured as such for the next few centuries during the Medieval Ages giving men and women the sense of connection and spiritual nourishment they craved and without which life, however rich in material wealth, is empty and meaningless.

It may be useful to trace the example of the decline of Rome and the rise of Christianity and the lessons this teaches us in today's world when a global market place richer and more extensive than any imagined in history because of technological improvements in communication, transportation, and otherwise has emerged. Yet it is interesting to note that this has not necessarily strengthened collectivistic bonds. It is true that no particular country can like Rome gain ascendancy in this sphere. While the West, America and Europe once commanded supremacy in this sphere, other markets Chinese, Indian, Japanese, Brazilian, etc., have come into competitive play. However, the globalization of the market has not necessarily produced global collectivization. On the contrary the division between the have's and have not's has widened as fewer people enjoy the benefits of global markets in terms of commodities or employment opportunities. Governments and their socialistic programs cannot effectively provide shelter against these economic adversities as they may once have, and many in fact have been scaled back to promote competitive success to their local financial and industrial enterprises in the international market place. In this sense, the Christian solution which emphasized restructuring the market and its commodities from a spiritual rather than a materialistic point of view as a way of achieving collectivity may prove an interesting historical example.

❧ CHAPTER VI ❧

Weapons: The Anti-Collectivistic Tool

It may be useful to focus on weapons and their relation to commodities though the boundaries between the two in the market place as presently constituted are hard to distinguish.

Commodities are essentially multidirectional since by definition they are meant to be shared with others binding the participants into a collectivity. If we like, we can represent a commodity by a set of lines that go in many different directions all at once. We mentioned the Thanksgiving Turkey that derives its value precisely because it is eaten on the same day throughout America and imparts a sense of a common identity and history to the millions consuming it, connecting them with one another geographically and also historically to previous and successive generations. It is obvious then that if one partakes of the Thanksgiving meal one realizes that other people are participating in it too.

Unlike commodities, weapons are directional. They emanate from one point in the time-space continuum and end in another. It is one thing for "A" to aim an arrow from a certain point in the space time continuum towards "B" situated at another point, and quite another for the arrow to come from "B" to "A." The same is true of more sophisticated weapons like bombs in modern warfare that are rained from overhead on their targets, adding air as a new dimensionality in the theater of war.

Each weapon will of course generate an anti or counter weapon from the person on the other side of the trajectory but the use of the weapon and of the consequent counter weapon, however quickly and frequently following one another, represents two distinct discreet moments in the time-space continuum.

The process will end only either:

As a stalemate where either side suspends all militaristic activity as futile

Where one side submits to the other acknowledging its domination as a way of avoiding further harm.

It is probable that all forms of domination whether along national, racial, ethnic, religious, sexual lines that have existed throughout history are due to the use of weaponry.

Throughout history the technology of weaponry has progressed and improved resulting in ever-greater capacity for violence and destruction, resulting in ever-greater forms of power. To give but a few examples: Witness the dominance of Rome over the nations bordering the rim of the Mediterranean—the ability of England through its use of a superior technology to extend its imperial designs over practically every corner of the world—the successful efforts of Nazi Germany and Communist Russia to bring much of Europe under their heels during World War II and shortly after.

Similar conquests along non-national lines involving sexual, racial, religious, ethnic and other lines of demarcation are equally notable and impressive—some forms of domination lasting a short time, some for hundreds and even thousands of years, and all resulting from the use of a superior weaponry and the accommodations which it achieved and necessitated.

The ultimate conclusion of weaponry development has of course been the Atom Bomb first used in World War II at Hiroshima and Nagasaki, and now sought after by an ever-growing number of nations.

Is the Atom Bomb a weapon?

In Nature, there are certain processes which if accelerated and carried beyond a certain point will have a different effect from one that is anticipated, as positives are inverted into negatives and negatives conversely into positives.

Is this true of the Atom Bomb that in contrast to a regular weapon it is no longer directional but like a commodity becomes multi-dimensional affecting both its user and its intended target?

True when the Atom Bomb was first used it victimized only the Japanese—the Americans and the rest of the world were immune to its effect as they had been in any former militaristic campaign. However at this juncture the potency of atomic power has escalated to a point where such directionality becomes obsolete and impossible to achieve.

The arrow symbol that symbolized a vectorial direction all weapons possessed can no longer be used to describe the ultimate weapon that has been developed.

In effect, the oppressor to the degree that he seeks to degrade the victim can never threaten to escalate the conflict to the point where the victim will submit as an accommodation since at a certain point the principle of escalation will result in a parity rather than disparity between the two. If anything escalation, the oppressor's ace in the hole, works on the victim's behalf.

Since Hiroshima and Nagasaki the space-time continuum on which military action is predicated has been transformed, warped and inverted to the point where warfare and the principle of escalation it involves no longer make sense.

It is true that in any conflict a superior power may engage in as we have been in Korea and Vietnam it may seek to de-escalate and only use a smaller or inferior technology where it will still have the advantage. But observe that since in the theater of war everyone knows that to ultimately win the superior power must escalate, and that such escalation no longer is possible, it is deprived of any advantages it may have. Hence since World War II no war whether in Korea or Vietnam has ever ended in the real sense of the word. If we are at war in Afghanistan as we were in Iraq the concept of a lasting peace secured by a peace treaty is no longer a viable resolution.

While it is no longer feasible for any country including our own, the only Super Power left, to achieve dominance, it is possible that the development of atomic weaponry may have worked retroactively to undo all forms of dominance however long ago they were imposed—whether by whites on Blacks, or men or women, to give but two examples—given that the accommodations they were based on are no longer plausible and credible.

Another corollary of what we are trying to say along sociological rather than geographical and military lines is that the Atomic Bomb has also had a radicalizing view of how we view others. In the past, the oppressor saw the oppressed as a distinct species of humanity whom he not only could subjugate but had every right to subjugate. Every conquest sprang from this sense of "otherness" and reinforced it in turn. When the Romans paraded their victims in Rome after every successful triumph, this reinforced their sense of Manifest Destiny that they had an almost divine right to rule the world and subjugate others, and punish by the most execrable methods any attempt on the part of the oppressed to rebel against their rule.

While the military parades and celebrations whereby we have toasted our military victories have been characterized by a triumphalist spirit, could the same kind of effect have taken place in the United States or anywhere in the world after we viewed the ravaging effects of Hiroshima and Nagasaki? Would anyone have delighted in the scenes of tens of thousands human literally consigned to Hell in one split moment of time? Instead of proving their otherness, did not the scenes of mammoth destruction remind us of their humanity and common ties to us, as they had become victims of an undeserved and terrifying fate which neither side could control, filling us with remorse and guilt rather than pride and triumph?

Two thousand years ago, with the establishment of Christianity, the sight of a man hanging on the Cross, helpless, powerless, reduced to the grossest form of suffering, indicated how the supreme weapon, the Cross, was transformed into an anti-weapon achieving the opposite of what it was intended for.

Is it possible that the Atomic Bomb constitutes its own counter weapon undoing the effect it was designed to accomplish and in some paradoxical way has been transformed into an anti-weapon and even a commodity?

It is impossible to predict the outcome of a nuclear weaponry that has transformed that space-time continuum on which all military ventures and their justification were based into a magnetic field where all the parts cohere and are parts of a larger integrated whole. The end is not remotely in sight. Nations still compete for the deadly power of nuclear weaponry, and are willing to sacrifice enormous money to achieve this end as well as risk universal sanction and opprobrium. Meanwhile this weaponry spreads to ever and ever smaller groups which have utter disdain for the concept of accommodation and can hold the world hostage if their demands are not met. Borders which are part of the space-time continuum and now melt in the magnetic field the atom bomb has created can no longer guarantee protection. It is only in the emergence of a shared sense of humanity and the archetypes that this translates into acting literally and metaphorically as the basis of an authentic marketplace where swords are beaten into plowshares which can avoid the dire consequences of a process that Hiroshima and Nagasaki have started. The die has been cast. The outcome remains to be seen.